Chinese New Year

Level 0 – Lilac

BookLife Readers

©2021 BookLife Publishing Ltd.
King's Lynn, Norfolk PE30 4LS

ISBN 978-1-83927-892-1

All rights reserved. Printed in England.
A catalogue record for this book is available
from the British Library.

Chinese New Year
Written by William Anthony
Designed by Amy Li

An Introduction to BookLife Readers...

Our Readers have been specifically created in line with the London Institute of Education's approach to book banding and are phonetically decodable and ordered to support each phase of Letters and Sounds.

Each book has been created to provide the best possible reading and learning experience. Our aim is to share our love of books with children, providing both emerging readers and prolific page-turners with beautiful books that are guaranteed to provoke interest and learning, regardless of ability.

BOOK BAND GRADED using the Institute of Education's approach to levelling.

PHONETICALLY DECODABLE supporting each phase of Letters and Sounds.

EXERCISES AND QUESTIONS to offer reinforcement and to ascertain comprehension.

CLEAR DESIGN to inspire and provoke engagement, providing the reader with clear visual representations of each non-fiction topic.

**AUTHOR INSIGHT:
WILLIAM ANTHONY**

Despite his young age, William Anthony's involvement with children's education is quite extensive. He has written over 60 titles with BookLife Publishing so far, across a wide range of subjects. William graduated from Cardiff University with a 1st Class BA (Hons) in Journalism, Media and Culture, creating an app and a TV series, among other things, during his time there.

William Anthony has also produced work for the Prince's Trust, a charity created by HRH The Prince of Wales, that helps young people with their professional future. He has created animated videos for a children's education company that works closely with the charity.

This book focuses on inspiring imagination and interest. This is a lilac level 0 book band.

Image Credits Images are courtesy of Shutterstock.com. With thanks to Getty Images, Thinkstock Photo and iStockphoto. Cover – KK Tan, JIANG HONGYAN, hareluya, Anirut Krisanakul, Tanachot Srijam, p4–5 – aslysun, elwynn, p6–7 – Toa55, windmoon, p8–9 – Tanachot Srijam, SKY2015, p10–11 – Anirut Krisanakul.

About Reading

When we read a book, we go from left to right, like this:

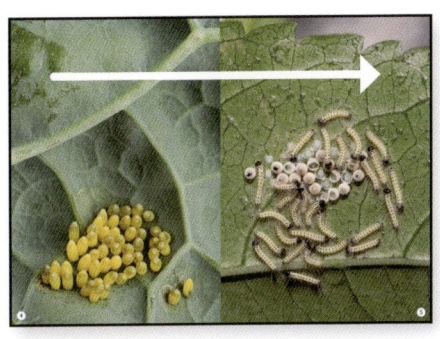

Some books just have pictures, like this:

Some books have words and pictures, like this:

Which photo shows somebody holding something?

BookLife Non-Fiction Readers

EXPLORE A WORLD OF NON-FICTION WITH OUR DECODABLE READER RANGE

Caterpillar to Butterfly
9781839278938

Chinese New Year
9781839278921

Dig a Pit
9781839278945

Tap the Puck
9781839278952

Pets
9781839278976

Picnic
9781839278969

Queens and Kings
9781839278990

Vets
9781839278983

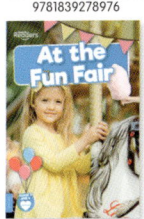
At the Fun Fair
9781839279010

Look Up!
9781839279003

At the Shop
9781839279027

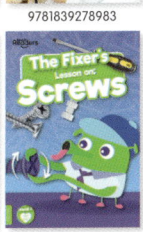
The Fixer's Lesson on: Screws
9781839279034

Stay Safe Online
9781839279058

Habitats
9781839279041

MORE COMING SOON

BookLife PUBLISHING

BookLife Readers

The BookLife Readers begin with the very basics of **phonetically decodable reading**. Starting with the earliest step of **CVC** words – words comprising a consonant, a vowel and a consonant – and building on this combination slowly, the reader follows a prescribed format taken directly from the recognised **Letters and Sounds** educational document.

By aligning our books with Letters and Sounds, we offer our readers a consistent approach to learning, whether at home or in the classroom. Books levelled as 'a' are an introduction to the band. Readers can advance to 'b' where graphemes are consolidated and further graphemes are introduced. The illustrations guide the reader, helping to deliver reading progression through the scheme in a **colourful** and **exciting** way. As a reader moves through the book band levels, the page numbers, level of repetition and sentence structure complexity all advance at a rate which **encourages development** without halting enjoyment.

To find out more about this exciting new reading scheme, visit **www.booklife.co.uk**